2017 SQA Past Papers with Answers

Higher
FRENCH

FREE
audio files to accompany this
title can be accessed at
**www.hoddereducation.co.uk/
sqaaudiofiles**
You will find the files listed by
language and level.

2015, 2016 & 2017 Exams

Hodder Gibson Study Skills Advice – General	– page 3
Hodder Gibson Study Skills Advice – Higher French	– page 5
2015 EXAM	– page 7
2016 EXAM	– page 33
2017 EXAM	– page 59
ANSWERS	– page 87

**HODDER
GIBSON**
AN HACHETTE UK COMPANY

This book contains the official 2015, 2016 and 2017 Exams for Higher French, with associated SQA-approved answers modified from the official marking instructions that accompany the paper.

In addition the book contains study skills advice. This advice has been specially commissioned by Hodder Gibson, and has been written by experienced senior teachers and examiners in line with the Higher for CfE syllabus and assessment outlines. This is not SQA material but has been devised to provide further guidance for Higher examinations.

Every effort has been made to trace the copyright holders and to obtain their permission for the use of copyright material. Hodder Gibson will be happy to receive information allowing us to rectify any error or omission in future editions.

Hachette UK's policy is to use papers that are natural, renewable and recyclable products and made from wood grown in sustainable forests. The logging and manufacturing processes are expected to conform to the environmental regulations of the country of origin.

Orders: please contact Bookpoint Ltd, 130 Park Drive, Milton Park, Abingdon, Oxon OX14 4SE. Telephone: (44) 01235 827720. Fax: (44) 01235 400454. Lines are open 9.00–5.00, Monday to Saturday, with a 24-hour message answering service. Visit our website at www.hoddereducation.co.uk. Hodder Gibson can be contacted direct on: Tel: 0141 333 4650; Fax: 0141 404 8188; email: hoddergibson@hodder.co.uk

This collection first published in 2017 by
Hodder Gibson, an imprint of Hodder Education,
An Hachette UK Company
211 St Vincent Street
Glasgow G2 5QY

Typeset by Aptara, Inc.

Printed in the UK

A catalogue record for this title is available from the British Library

ISBN: 978-1-5104-2147-9

2 1

2018 2017

MIX
Paper from
responsible sources
FSC™ C104740

Introduction

Study Skills – what you need to know to pass exams!

Pause for thought

Many students might skip quickly through a page like this. After all, we all know how to revise. Do you really though?

Think about this:

"IF YOU ALWAYS DO WHAT YOU ALWAYS DO, YOU WILL ALWAYS GET WHAT YOU HAVE ALWAYS GOT."

Do you like the grades you get? Do you want to do better? If you get full marks in your assessment, then that's great! Change nothing! This section is just to help you get that little bit better than you already are.

There are two main parts to the advice on offer here. The first part highlights fairly obvious things but which are also very important. The second part makes suggestions about revision that you might not have thought about but which WILL help you.

Part 1

DOH! It's so obvious but …

Start revising in good time

Don't leave it until the last minute – this will make you panic.

Make a revision timetable that sets out work time AND play time.

Sleep and eat!

Obvious really, and very helpful. Avoid arguments or stressful things too – even games that wind you up. You need to be fit, awake and focused!

Know your place!

Make sure you know exactly **WHEN and WHERE** your exams are.

Know your enemy!

Make sure you know what to expect in the exam.

How is the paper structured?

How much time is there for each question?

What types of question are involved?

Which topics seem to come up time and time again?

Which topics are your strongest and which are your weakest?

Are all topics compulsory or are there choices?

Learn by DOING!

There is no substitute for past papers and practice papers – they are simply essential! Tackling this collection of papers and answers is exactly the right thing to be doing as your exams approach.

Part 2

People learn in different ways. Some like low light, some bright. Some like early morning, some like evening/night. Some prefer warm, some prefer cold. But everyone uses their BRAIN and the brain works when it is active. Passive learning – sitting gazing at notes – is the most INEFFICIENT way to learn anything. Below you will find tips and ideas for making our revision more effectice and maybe even more enjoyable. What follows gets your brain active, and active learning works!

Activity 1 – Stop and review

Step 1

When you have done no more than 5 minutes of revision reading STOP!

Step 2

Write a heading in your own words which sums up the topic you have been revising.

Step 3

Write a summary of what you have revised in no more than two sentences. Don't fool yourself by saying, "I know it, but I cannot put it into words". That just means you don't know it well enough. If you cannot write your summary, revise that section again, knowing that you must write a summary at the end of it. Many of you will have notebooks full of blue/black ink writing. Many of the pages will not be especially attractive or memorable so try to liven them up a bit with colour as you are reviewing and rewriting. **This is a great memory aid, and memory is the most important thing.**

Activity 2 – Use technology!

Why should everything be written down? Have you thought about "mental" maps, diagrams, cartoons and colour to help you learn? And rather than write down notes, why not record your revision material?

What about having a text message revision session with friends? Keep in touch with them to find out how and what they are revising and share ideas and questions.

Why not make a video diary where you tell the camera what you are doing, what you think you have learned and what you still have to do? No one has to see or hear it, but the process of having to organise your thoughts in a formal way to explain something is a very important learning practice.

Be sure to make use of electronic files. You could begin to summarise your class notes. Your typing might be slow, but it will get faster and the typed notes will be easier to read than the scribbles in your class notes. Try to add different fonts and colours to make your work stand out. You can easily Google relevant pictures, cartoons and diagrams which you can copy and paste to make your work more attractive and **MEMORABLE**.

Activity 3 – This is it. Do this and you will know lots!

Step 1

In this task you must be very honest with yourself! Find the SQA syllabus for your subject (www.sqa.org.uk). Look at how it is broken down into main topics called MANDATORY knowledge. That means stuff you MUST know.

Step 2

BEFORE you do ANY revision on this topic, write a list of everything that you already know about the subject. It might be quite a long list but you only need to write it once. It shows you all the information that is already in your long-term memory so you know what parts you do not need to revise!

Step 3

Pick a chapter or section from your book or revision notes. Choose a fairly large section or a whole chapter to get the most out of this activity.

With a buddy, use Skype, Facetime, Twitter or any other communication you have, to play the game "If this is the answer, what is the question?". For example, if you are revising Geography and the answer you provide is "meander", your buddy would have to make up a question like "What is the word that describes a feature of a river where it flows slowly and bends often from side to side?".

Make up 10 "answers" based on the content of the chapter or section you are using. Give this to your buddy to solve while you solve theirs.

Step 4

Construct a wordsearch of at least 10 × 10 squares. You can make it as big as you like but keep it realistic. Work together with a group of friends. Many apps allow you to make wordsearch puzzles online. The words and phrases can go in any direction and phrases can be split. Your puzzle must only contain facts linked to the topic you are revising. Your task is to find 10 bits of information to hide in your puzzle, but you must not repeat information that you used in Step 3. DO NOT show where the words are. Fill up empty squares with random letters. Remember to keep a note of where your answers are hidden but do not show your friends. When you have a complete puzzle, exchange it with a friend to solve each other's puzzle.

Step 5

Now make up 10 questions (not "answers" this time) based on the same chapter used in the previous two tasks. Again, you must find NEW information that you have not yet used. Now it's getting hard to find that new information! Again, give your questions to a friend to answer.

Step 6

As you have been doing the puzzles, your brain has been actively searching for new information. Now write a NEW LIST that contains only the new information you have discovered when doing the puzzles. Your new list is the one to look at repeatedly for short bursts over the next few days. Try to remember more and more of it without looking at it. After a few days, you should be able to add words from your second list to your first list as you increase the information in your long-term memory.

FINALLY! Be inspired...

Make a list of different revision ideas and beside each one write **THINGS I HAVE** tried, **THINGS I WILL** try and **THINGS I MIGHT** try. Don't be scared of trying something new.

And remember – "FAIL TO PREPARE AND PREPARE TO FAIL!"

Higher French

The course

The Higher French course aims to enable you to develop the ability to:

- read, listen, talk and write in French
- understand and use French
- apply your knowledge and understanding of the language.

The course offers the opportunity to develop detailed language skills in the real-life contexts of society, learning, employability and culture.

How the course is graded

The course assessment will take the form of a performance and a written exam:

- The performance will be a presentation and discussion with your teacher, which will be recorded and marked by your teacher. This is out of 30, and makes up 30% of your final mark.
- The written exam will be sat in May. This book will help you practise for the exam.

The exams

Reading and Directed Writing

- exam time: 1 hour 40 minutes

Reading

- total marks: 30
- weighting in final grade: 30%
- what you have to do: read a passage of about 600 words, and answer questions about it in English, including an overall purpose question for 20 marks; translate an extract from the passage of about 40 words into English for 10 marks.

Directed Writing

- total marks: 10
- weighting in final grade: 10%
- what you have to do: write 120–150 words in French describing a visit you made, or an experience you had, in a French speaking country.

Listening and Personal Response Writing

- exam time: 60 minutes
- total marks: 30
- weighting in final grade: 30%
- what you have to do: Section 1 (20 marks): listen to a presentation in French, and answer questions about it in English; then listen to a conversation In French, and answer questions about it in English. Section 2 (10 marks): write 120–150 words in

French as a personal response to the topic discussed in the conversation: there will be three specific questions to be addressed.

How to improve your mark!

Reading

- Read the whole passage, then pick out the key points. Detailed answers are generally required, so pay particular attention to words like assez, très, trop, vraiment and to negatives. Make sure you get the details of numbers, days, times etc. right.
- Use the line numbers above each question to guide you as to where to look for the answer.
- Take care when using dictionaries where a word has more than one meaning. Learn to choose the correct meaning from a list of meanings in a dictionary, and get in the habit of going beyond the headword. Often you will find the whole phrase you are looking for further down the entry.
- Try to answer the specific wording of the question, but do not give a word-for-word translation of the text as a response to the reading comprehension questions, as this often results in an answer which is not in correct English.
- When responding to the questions in the Reading papers, you should be guided by the number of points awarded for each question. You should give as much detail in your answer as you have understood, but should not put down everything which is in the original text, as you are wasting time. The question itself usually indicates the amount of information required by stating in bold, e.g. 'State **two** of them'. If the question says 'Give **any two**', there are more than two possibilities, so choose the two you are happiest with and stick to them.
- The last question before the translation asks you to look at the passage as a whole, then answer a question and provide evidence to back up your answer. It is important to start your answer with your opinion, then select pieces of text from the passage to back up your answer, giving an English version of what is in the passage.
- Look closely at each word in each section of the translation passage, and pay particular attention to the articles and tenses used. Make sure you include each word in your translation (although translation is not word for word!). Look at marking schemes for translations to give you an idea of what a good translation should look like.

Directed Writing

- Have a quick look at the two choices for writing, and go for the one for which your prepared material will give you most support.

- Consider, carefully, the wording of each bullet point, and make sure any learned material that you use is relevant and appropriate to the bullet point. Make sure you address each part of the first bullet point, and that you are answering the questions asked.

- Use your dictionary only to check the accuracy of what you have written (spelling, genders etc.), not to create and invent new sentences.

- Don't write pieces that are too lengthy, you only need 120–150 words. So stick to 30–40 words per bullet point.

- Be aware of the extended criteria to be used in assessing performances in Writing (included on pages 90–92 and pages 93–95 of this book!) so that you know what's required to achieve the good and very good categories in terms of content, accuracy, and range and variety of language.

- Ensure that your handwriting is legible (particularly when writing in French) and distinguish clearly between rough notes and what you wish to be considered as final answers. Make sure you score out your notes!

- You should bear the following points in mind:

  - There are four bullet points to answer: they are not really predictable and vary from year to year, but certain things come up regularly.

  - Each of the four bullet points should have between 30 and 40 words to address it properly.

  - You will be assessed on how well you have answered the points, and on the accuracy of your language.

  - If you miss out or fail to address a bullet point correctly, the most you can get is six marks.

  - For a mark of good or very good, you should have some complex language such as longer, varied sentences, adjectives and conjunctions.

Listening

- Your listening skills will improve most with practice. So use the Listening sections in this book several times to get used to the format of the exam.

- Read the questions carefully before the first listening and use them as a means of anticipating the sort of information you will need to extract from the text.

- Not giving enough detail is still a major reason for candidates losing marks. Many answers are correct as far as they go, but don't have enough detail to score marks. The same rules as for Reading apply. Give as much detail as possible in your answers and don't lose marks by writing down numbers, prepositions and question words inaccurately.

- You hear each of the two Listening texts twice only, so make use of the gap between the two recordings to check which specific details you still need for your answers, so your listening is focused.

- Make sure you're able to give accurate answers through confident knowledge of numbers, common adjectives, weather expressions, prepositions and question words, so that some of the 'easier' points of information are not lost through lack of sufficiently accurate details.

- When responding to the questions in the Listening papers, be guided by the number of points awarded for each question, and by the wording of the question. You should give as much detail in your answer as you have understood, but should not write down everything you hear. The question itself usually indicates the amount of information required by stating in bold, e.g. 'Give **2** of them'.

- Be sure to put a line through any notes you have made!

Personal Response Writing

- Make sure you read the stimulus questions carefully and adapt any learned material you use so it's relevant to the aspects contained in them.

- There are three questions to be answered and you must answer them all, at roughly the same length. Aim for 40–50 words for each of them.

- Don't be tempted to rewrite an answer you have written on the topic previously: you have to be sure your answer is relevant to the questions put to you.

Good luck!

Remember that the rewards for passing Higher French are well worth it! Your pass will help you get the future you want for yourself. In the exam, be confident in your own ability. If you're not sure how to answer a question, trust your instincts and just give it a go anyway – keep calm and don't panic! GOOD LUCK!

HIGHER

2015

National
Qualifications
2015

X730/76/11

**French
Reading**

FRIDAY, 22 MAY

1:00 PM – 2:40 PM

Total marks — 30

Attempt ALL questions.

Write your answers clearly, in **English**, in the Reading Answer Booklet provided. In the answer booklet you must clearly identify the question number you are attempting.

You may use a French dictionary.

Use **blue** or **black** ink.

There is a separate question and answer booklet for Directed Writing. You must complete your answer for Directed Writing in the question and answer booklet for Directed Writing.

Before leaving the examination room you must give your Reading Answer Booklet and your Directed Writing question and answer booklet to the Invigilator; if you do not, you may lose all the marks for this paper.

Total marks — 30

Attempt ALL questions

Read the whole article carefully and then answer, in **English**, ALL the questions that follow.

This article discusses modern technology.

La Technologie Moderne

Depuis quelques années, la technologie a évolué très rapidement. En effet, la technologie fait maintenant partie de notre vie quotidienne que ce soit au niveau des ordinateurs ou des téléphones portables. Elle nous est utile tous les jours à l'école, mais aussi au travail. Comparé à la console de jeux ou à l'ordinateur, le téléphone portable est l'objet
5 électronique par excellence. Le portable représente pour la majorité des jeunes un objet de prestige et de statut social, quelque chose qu'ils utilisent pour définir leur personnalité.

Ainsi, un ado sur 20 développe des symptômes de dépendance. Certains vont même jusqu'à prendre l'appareil sous la douche. Les «accros» ne dorment pas assez et par
10 conséquent, ils ont de moins bons résultats scolaires. En plus, les relations avec leurs parents sont souvent tendues. Bref, ils consacrent une bonne partie de leur temps au téléphone portable.

Mais pourquoi les jeunes sont-ils si «accros» à leur téléphone portable ?
Le portable semble devenir indispensable pour les jeunes de 12 à 18 ans. Certains d'entre
15 eux affirment se sentir «nu» sans leur portable et ne pas savoir comment vivre sans lui. D'autres déclarent en avoir honte parce que l'appareil est devenu trop vieux. La plupart des ados considèrent leur portable comme leur meilleur ami. Les portables sont souvent équipés de fonctions ultra-performantes. Ils permettent aux jeunes non seulement d'envoyer des textos, mais aussi de télécharger de la musique achetée en ligne, et, dans
20 une moindre mesure de jouer à des jeux préinstallés.

La peur d'être séparé de son téléphone portable
Beaucoup de jeunes dorment avec leur téléphone portable allumé sous leur oreiller ou le posent sur une table de chevet pour qu'il soit juste à côté de leur lit parce qu'ils veulent être contactés à tout moment.

25 Matthieu, âgé de 15 ans, nous raconte: «j'ai eu mon premier portable à 12 ans. Je l'utilise chaque jour sans exception. Je me lève et je me couche avec mon portable, je ne peux pas m'en passer. Il faut absolument que je consulte mes textos et mes emails constamment. Ne me demandez pas de passer 30 minutes sans mon téléphone, je n'y arriverai pas».

30 **Les SMS sont partout**
Les SMS permettent de communiquer avec plusieurs personnes en même temps. Ils sont d'ailleurs devenus plus privés que les coups de fils et certains se servent de cette méthode pour envoyer un texto discrètement même au cinéma. Toutefois, cette écriture d'un genre particulier inquiète certains adultes.

35 Mme Lambert, enseignante du secondaire explique: «Je pense que les textos sont en train de détruire la capacité des jeunes à bien s'exprimer quand ils écrivent. Comme ils écrivent dans le langage SMS, les élèves ont tendance à négliger leur grammaire et cela se reflète beaucoup dans leurs études.

Même mon fils Philippe envoie une centaine de SMS par jour. Il trouve ça plus rapide, plus
40 efficace et il peut envoyer un SMS tout en faisant autre chose en même temps. Ça m'énerve.» Mais cela n'a aucune signification pour la plupart des jeunes. Philippe dit: «Mon portable est essentiel dans ma vie.»

MARKS

Questions

Re-read lines 1–12.

1. The writer discusses mobile phones.

   (a) What does the mobile phone represent for the majority of young people?   2

   (b) What evidence is there that some young people are addicted to their phone?   1

   (c) In what way does this addiction affect their everyday life? Give any **two** details.   2

Re-read lines 13–16.

2. The article further describes the nature of this "addiction".
   What examples does the writer give? State any **two**.   2

Re-read lines 21–29.

3. Many young people are frightened of being separated from their phone.

   (a) In what ways does the writer highlight this?   2

   (b) What shows that Matthieu relies heavily on his phone? Give any **three** details.   3

Re-read lines 30–34.

4. The article then focuses on text messaging.
   What are the advantages of text messaging?   3

Re-read lines 35–42.

5. The article discusses some concerns adults have about text messaging.

   (a) What are Mme Lambert's concerns?   2

   (b) What does her son Philippe do that annoys her?   1

6. Now consider the article as a whole.

   Does the writer give a more positive or negative view of the use of mobile phones amongst young people? Give reasons for your answer with reference to the text.   2

7. Translate into English the underlined section.
   «La plupart . . . préinstallés.» (lines 17–20)   10

[END OF QUESTION PAPER]

Page three

[BLANK PAGE]

DO NOT WRITE ON THIS PAGE

H

National
Qualifications
2015

Mark

X730/76/02

**French
Directed Writing**

FRIDAY, 22 MAY

1:00 PM — 2:40 PM

Fill in these boxes and read what is printed below.

Full name of centre

Town

Forename(s)

Surname

Number of seat

Date of birth

Day   Month   Year

Scottish candidate number

Total marks — 10

Choose ONE scenario on *Page two* and write your answer clearly, in **French**, in the space provided in this booklet. You must clearly identify the scenario number you are attempting.

You may use a French dictionary.

Additional space for answers is provided at the end of this booklet.

Use **blue** or **black** ink.

There is a separate answer booklet for Reading. You must complete your answers for Reading in the answer booklet for Reading.

Before leaving the examination room you must give this Directed Writing question and answer booklet and your Reading Answer Booklet to the Invigilator; if you do not, you may lose all the marks for this paper.

MARKS | DO NOT WRITE IN THIS MARGIN

Total marks — 10

Choose **one** of the following two scenarios.

SCENARIO 1: Employability

> Last summer you spent three weeks working in a hotel in France. On your return you have been asked to write an account **in French** of your experience for the hotel's website.

You must include the following information and **you should try to add** other relevant details:

- Where the hotel was located **and** what it was like
- What you liked/disliked about the job
- How you got on with your colleagues
- Whether or not you would recommend working abroad to others

You should write approximately 120 – 150 words.

OR

SCENARIO 2: Culture

> Last year you went to France to stay with a French family.
> On your return you have been asked to write an account **in French** for the French family's local newspaper.

You must include the following information and **you should try to add** other relevant details:

- Where in France the family lived **and** how you travelled there
- What you did with the family at the weekend
- What differences you noticed between the French and Scottish way of life
- Whether you would recommend living with a family in another country

You should write approximately 120 – 150 words.

ANSWER SPACE

Scenario number

ANSWER SPACE (continued)

MARKS | DO NOT WRITE IN THIS MARGIN

ANSWER SPACE (continued)

ANSWER SPACE (continued)

MARKS | DO NOT WRITE IN THIS MARGIN

[END OF QUESTION PAPER]

ADDITIONAL SPACE FOR ANSWERS

MARKS | DO NOT WRITE IN THIS MARGIN

MARKS | DO NOT WRITE IN THIS MARGIN

ADDITIONAL SPACE FOR ANSWERS

H

National Qualifications 2015

Mark

X730/76/03

**French
Listening and Writing**

FRIDAY, 22 MAY

3:00 PM – 4:00 PM

Fill in these boxes and read what is printed below.

Full name of centre

Town

Forename(s)

Surname

Number of seat

Date of birth

Day   Month   Year

Scottish candidate number

Total marks — 30

SECTION 1 — LISTENING — 20 marks.

You will hear two items in French. **Before you hear each item, you will have one minute to study the question.** You will hear each item twice, with an interval of one minute between playings. You will then have time to answer the questions before hearing the next item. Write your answers clearly, in **English**, in the spaces provided.

SECTION 2 — WRITING — 10 marks.

Write your answer clearly, in **French**, in the space provided.

Attempt ALL questions. You may use a French dictionary.

Additional space for answers is provided at the end of this booklet. If you use this space you must clearly identify the question number you are attempting.

You are not allowed to leave the examination room until the end of the test.

Use **blue** or **black** ink.

Before leaving the examination room you must give this booklet to the Invigilator; if you do not, you may lose all the marks for this paper.

MARKS | DO NOT WRITE IN THIS MARGIN

SECTION 1 — LISTENING — 20 marks

Attempt ALL questions

Item 1

Valérie talks about her experience of learning languages at school in France.

(a)   (i)   What is the advantage of using tablet computers according to Valérie?

1

_____

(ii)   What kinds of activities do pupils do in class with tablet computers? State any **two** things.

2

_____

_____

(b)   The languages teachers often use the interactive whiteboard. What are the benefits of this?

2

_____

_____

(c)   Valérie talks about a school trip to England.

Why was it easy and practical as a destination?

2

_____

_____

(d)   Consider Valérie's talk as a whole. Overall, which of the following statements best reflects her experience at school?

1

	Tick (✓)
Valérie never uses technology in language classes.	
Valérie is positive about the use of technology in language classes.	
Valérie's language teachers are not confident in using technology.	

Item 2

MARKS | DO NOT WRITE IN THIS MARGIN

Nicole talks to Christophe about the importance of languages to her future career.

(a) In what ways is Nicole's school different from other schools?

1

_____

(b) What are the advantages of living near the border?

2

_____

_____

(c) (i) Nicole is planning to do a work-placement abroad.

When is she planning to do this?

1

_____

(ii) She will gain experience of the world of work.

What else does she hope to gain from this?

1

_____

(d) What will she do to organise her work-placement? State any **three** things.

3

_____

_____

_____

_____

(e) What are Nicole's plans after she leaves university?

2

_____

_____

_____

(f) In Nicole's opinion, why is it important to study languages nowadays? State any **one** thing.

1

_____

(g) What are the advantages of being bilingual?

1

_____

[Turn over

Page three

MARKS | DO NOT WRITE IN THIS MARGIN

SECTION 2 — WRITING — 10 marks

Nicole nous a parlé de l'importance des langues. Est-ce que les langues sont importantes pour toi? Est-ce que tu voudrais faire un stage à l'étranger? Pourquoi/pourquoi pas?

Écris 120 – 150 mots pour exprimer tes idées.

_____

_____

_____

_____

_____

_____

_____

_____

_____

_____

_____

_____

_____

_____

_____

_____

_____

_____

_____

ANSWER SPACE FOR SECTION 2 (continued)

MARKS DO NOT WRITE IN THIS MARGIN

ANSWER SPACE FOR SECTION 2 (continued)

[END OF QUESTION PAPER]

MARKS | DO NOT WRITE IN THIS MARGIN

ADDITIONAL SPACE FOR ANSWERS

MARKS | DO NOT WRITE IN THIS MARGIN

ADDITIONAL SPACE FOR ANSWERS

Page eight

National
Qualifications
2015

X730/76/13

French
Listening Transcript

FRIDAY, 22 MAY

3:00 PM – 4:00 PM

This paper must not be seen by any candidate.

The material overleaf is provided for use in an emergency only (eg the recording or equipment proving faulty) or where permission has been given in advance by SQA for the material to be read to candidates with additional support needs. The material must be read exactly as printed.

Instructions to reader(s):

For each item, read the English **once**, then read the French **twice**, with an interval of 1 minute between the two readings. On completion of the second reading, pause for the length of time indicated in brackets after the item, to allow the candidates to write their answers.

Where special arrangements have been agreed in advance to allow the reading of the material, those sections marked **(f)** should be read by a female speaker and those marked **(m)** by a male; those sections marked **(t)** should be read by the teacher.

(t)   Item Number One

Valérie talks about her experience of learning languages at school in France.

You now have one minute to study the questions for Item Number One.

(f)   En général j'aime aller au lycée parce que j'y vois mes copines. Les cours qui m'intéressent le plus sont les langues vivantes. J'étudie l'anglais, l'espagnol et le mandarin. J'apprécie beaucoup la façon d'apprendre les langues au lycée. Tous les élèves ont un ordinateur portable ou une tablette donc on peut faire toutes sortes de choses. A mon avis les tablettes nous encouragent à prendre plus de responsabilités. Par exemple on peut filmer nos dialogues en classe et télécharger des jeux linguistiques. En plus on a l'occasion de pratiquer notre langue écrite tout en s'amusant parce que chaque mois on échange des emails avec nos correspondants à l'étranger.

Au lycée mes professeurs de langues utilisent aussi beaucoup de tableaux interactifs pour les compétitions en ligne. C'est très bénéfique pour tous les élèves qui sont très compétitifs et aiment gagner. Cela les encourage à travailler en équipe.

Il y a deux ans j'ai eu beaucoup de chance car mon lycée a organisé un voyage culturel d'une semaine en Angleterre. Il était facile et pratique d'aller en Angleterre car on habite dans le nord-est de la France donc le voyage n'était pas trop long et pas trop cher.

(2 minutes)

(t) Item Number Two

Nicole talks to Christophe about the importance of languages to her future career.

You now have one minute to study the questions for Item Number Two.

(m) **Nicole, tu apprends des langues à ton lycée. Qu'est-ce que tu en penses?**

(f) Je dois dire que mon lycée est très différent des autres lycées de la région. J'habite dans une grande ville tout près de la frontière italienne. Donc il y a beaucoup d'élèves dans mon lycée avec qui on peut parler italien.

(m) **Est-ce que tu crois qu'il y a des avantages d'habiter près de la frontière?**

(f) Il est très facile d'aller en Italie parce que la ville italienne la plus proche est à cinquante kilomètres de chez moi. Donc j'ai l'occasion d'améliorer ma connaissance de la langue en bavardant dans les cafés et aux marchés.

(m) **Tu as l'intention de continuer avec tes langues après le lycée?**

(f) Oui, j'ai l'intention de faire des études de commerce avec des langues. Quand je serai en troisième année à l'université j'aurai la possibilité de faire un stage à l'étranger.

(m) **Où est-ce que tu feras ton stage?**

(f) Je vais chercher un stage dans une compagnie italienne. Comme ça je gagnerai de l'expérience dans le monde du travail tout en gagnant de l'argent.

(m) **Mais comment vas-tu trouver des stages à l'étranger?**

(f) Je devrai contacter des compagnies durant ma deuxième année de fac. Certains professeurs à l'université ont une liste de compagnies qui prennent des jeunes étudiants. Mais en fin de compte c'est ma responsabilité d'organiser le stage, le transport et le logement. Je ferai aussi des recherches sur Internet. Ce sera un grand défi pour moi mais l'expérience sera sensationnelle.

(m) **Qu'est-ce que tu veux faire après l'université?**

(f) Moi je vais travailler le plus vite possible. Mais je ne sais pas exactement ce que je veux faire. Pour moi la chose la plus importante c'est de trouver un travail intéressant et d'utiliser mes langues dans le domaine du commerce.

(m) **Pourquoi est-il important de savoir parler une langue étrangère de nos jours?**

(f) Je trouve qu'étudier les langues étrangères est essentiel de nos jours. Ça élargit ses horizons et c'est indispensable dans le commerce et le tourisme. Mon but c'est de perfectionner mes langues car mon idéal serait d'être bilingue.

[Turn over

(m) Quels sont les avantages de parler deux langues à ton avis?

(f) Quand on parle deux langues on peut assister et contribuer à des conférences. Comme ça je peux utiliser mes connaissances linguistiques pour voyager dans le monde entier.

(t) End of recording.

[END OF TRANSCRIPT]

HIGHER

2016

National Qualifications 2016

X730/76/11

French Reading

MONDAY, 16 MAY

9:00 AM – 10:40 AM

Total marks — 30

Attempt ALL questions.

Write your answers clearly, in **English**, in the Reading answer booklet provided. In the answer booklet you must clearly identify the question number you are attempting.

You may use a French dictionary.

Use **blue** or **black** ink.

There is a separate question and answer booklet for Directed Writing. You must complete your answer for Directed Writing in the question and answer booklet for Directed Writing.

Before leaving the examination room you must give your Reading answer booklet and your Directed Writing question and answer booklet to the Invigilator; if you do not, you may lose all the marks for this paper.

Total marks — 30

Attempt ALL questions

Read the whole article carefully and then answer, in **English**, ALL the questions that follow.

This article talks about an increasingly popular type of film which features young people as the main character.

L'adolescent, héros de cinéma

Jennifer Lawrence, star du film *Hunger Games*, est l'acteur du moment. Elle a déjà joué dans plusieurs films. Si on l'aime beaucoup, c'est peut-être parce qu'elle est différente des autres jeunes acteurs. Elle a grandi loin de New-York, dans l'état du Kentucky. Elle pratiquait des sports avec ses grands frères tout en étant majorette dans son lycée. Elle n'a jamais pris de 5 cours de théâtre et aucun de ses parents ne travaille dans le cinéma.

Jennifer n'est pas la seule star de cinéma sur nos écrans. Chaque semaine ou presque, des douzaines de nouveaux films avec des héros adolescents sortent au cinéma. Même si ce n'est pas un nouveau phénomène, il s'est développé massivement pendant les vingt dernières années, par exemple dans les films *Warhorse* et *Chronicle*. Pendant cette période le héros 10 typique est devenu de plus en plus jeune, ce qui attire une nouvelle clientèle également jeune.

Le nouveau héros typique

Ces films illustrent que les jeunes héros sont partout dans les films. Les directeurs de cinéma se sont inspirés des problèmes des jeunes tels que la drogue, l'amour et le stress des 15 examens. Cependant il faut avouer que les adolescents qui se disputent avec des adultes n'est pas du tout un nouveau thème au cinéma. Le héros typique de ce genre de films est souvent indépendant et parfois un peu rebelle. Il ou elle ne respecte plus aucune règle. Les parents, de leur côté, sont souvent absents. Ils sont incapables de leur donner des limites ou parfois même, ils abandonnent leur rôle de parents car leurs journées de travail sont de plus 20 en plus longues et épuisantes. Par conséquent, les adolescents sont souvent laissés seuls à la maison.

L'opinion des jeunes

Mais que pensent les jeunes de la façon dont le cinéma contemporain les représente? Ce qu'ils n'aiment pas, c'est l'image de l'adolescent malheureux, isolé, solitaire, l'adolescent qui 25 ne sait pas communiquer avec ses camarades de classe ou les adultes autour de lui et qui passe tout son temps devant son écran d'ordinateur.

Rémi Laporte, 17 ans, au lycée Pablo Picasso à Perpignan ajoute: «Je n'aime pas les comédies françaises qui montrent des images clichés des adolescents comme leur immaturité, leur colère, leur mauvaise humeur».

30 Selon l'expert David Martin, sociologue à l'Université de Nantes ce que les jeunes préfèrent, ce sont les films qui mettent en scène des bandes d'adolescents parfois effrontés qui font des bêtises ensemble, ou des bandes d'amis qui s'aident et essaient de résoudre leurs problèmes. Ils admettent cependant qu'ils les regardent avec une certaine distance car elles ne reflètent pas vraiment l'adolescence d'aujourd'hui.

35 La perte de l'innocence

Dans le monde occidental, ces films ont souvent pour intention de refléter la vie quotidienne des jeunes et en particulier les relations difficiles avec les parents est un thème que l'on trouve partout dans les films populaires. Au contraire dans les pays en développement, la présence d'adolescents dans les films sert plutôt à dénoncer la guerre, la pauvreté ou les 40 inégalités. En plus les films montrent comment, dans une grande partie du monde, on grandit trop vite et l'enfant devient adulte sans jamais être adolescent.

Pour les cinéastes, il est difficile de trouver le bon équilibre entre la réalité et le fantasme pour plaire au grand public.

Page two

Questions   MARKS

Re-read lines 1—5.

1. In what ways is Jennifer Lawrence different from other young actors? State any **three** things.   3

Re-read lines 6—11.

2. The writer discusses the increase in the number of films where the main character is a teenager.

   (a) What shows that this type of film is becoming more popular?   1

   (b) How has the typical main character changed over the last 20 years?   1

   (c) What effect has this had on cinema-going?   1

Re-read lines 16—21.

3. The writer goes on to discuss the typical main character in these films.

   (a) The writer states that the main character is often independent and rebellious. What else does the writer state about the main character?   1

   (b) (i) Parents are often absent from the main character's life. What examples demonstrate this?   2

       (ii) What is the result?   1

Re-read lines 22—34.

4. Young people do not always react positively to the way in which cinema portrays them.

   (a) They are often seen as unhappy, isolated and lonely. What other aspects of their portrayal do they not like?   2

   (b) Rémi does not like the way French comedies represent young people.
       Give an example of this.   1

   (c) According to the sociologist David Martin, what kind of films do young people like to watch? State any **two** things   2

[Questions 5 to 7 are on *Page four*

MARKS

Questions (continued)

Re-read lines 35—43

5. There are differences between the portrayal of young people in western and in developing countries.

   (a) What themes do films reflect **in western countries**? State any **one** thing.   1

   (b)   (i) What is the main theme of films **in developing countries**?   1

          (ii) What else do these films show? State any **one** thing.   1

6. Now consider the article as a whole.

   In what way do film makers represent young people in film? Give details from the text to justify your answer.   2

7. Translate into English the underlined section.

   «Ces films . . . au cinéma» (lines 13—16)   10

[END OF QUESTION PAPER]

FOR OFFICIAL USE

H

National
Qualifications
2016

Mark

X730/76/02

French
Directed Writing

MONDAY, 16 MAY

9:00 AM – 10:40 AM

Fill in these boxes and read what is printed below.

Full name of centre

Town

Forename(s)

Surname

Number of seat

Date of birth

Day	Month	Year

Scottish candidate number

Total marks — 10

Choose ONE scenario on *Page two* and write your answer clearly, in **French**, in the space provided in this booklet. You must clearly identify the scenario number you are attempting.

You may use a French dictionary.

Additional space for answers is provided at the end of this booklet.

Use **blue** or **black** ink.

There is a separate answer booklet for Reading. You must complete your answers for Reading in the answer booklet for Reading.

Before leaving the examination room you must give this Directed Writing question and answer booklet and your Reading answer booklet to the Invigilator; if you do not, you may lose all the marks for this paper.

Total marks — 10

Choose **one** of the following two scenarios.

SCENARIO 1: Society

> Last summer you had the opportunity to spend two months in the south of France. During your stay you travelled to other parts of France. On your return you have been asked to write an account **in French** of your experience for your school/college website.

You must include the following information and **you should try to add** other relevant details:

- why you went to France **and** what the journey was like
- what you thought of the areas you visited
- what you liked/disliked about the French way of life
- whether you would recommend this type of experience

You should write approximately 120–150 words.

OR

SCENARIO 2: Learning

> Last year you went to France on an activities holiday with your school. During your stay you had the opportunity to try out some new sports and other activities. On your return you have been asked to write an account **in French** of your experience.

You must include the following information **and you should try to add** other relevant details:

- where exactly you went in France **and** who you went with
- what new sports or activities you took part in
- how you got on with the others taking part
- whether or not you would recommend this kind of holiday to others

You should write approximately 120–150 words.

ANSWER SPACE

MARKS | DO NOT WRITE IN THIS MARGIN

Scenario number [ ]

_____

_____

_____

_____

_____

_____

_____

_____

_____

_____

_____

_____

_____

_____

_____

_____

_____

_____

_____

_____

_____

_____

_____

_____

_____

_____

_____

_____

[Turn over

MARKS DO NOT WRITE IN THIS MARGIN

ANSWER SPACE (continued)

ANSWER SPACE (continued)

[Turn over

MARKS DO NOT WRITE IN THIS MARGIN

ANSWER SPACE (continued)

[END OF QUESTION PAPER]

MARKS | DO NOT WRITE IN THIS MARGIN

ADDITIONAL SPACE FOR ANSWERS

MARKS | DO NOT WRITE IN THIS MARGIN

ADDITIONAL SPACE FOR ANSWERS

H

National Qualifications 2016

Mark

X730/76/03

French
Listening and Writing

MONDAY, 16 MAY

11:00 AM – 12:00 NOON

Fill in these boxes and read what is printed below.

Full name of centre

Town

Forename(s)

Surname

Number of seat

Date of birth

Day   Month   Year

Scottish candidate number

Total marks — 30

SECTION 1 — LISTENING — 20 marks

You will hear two items in French. **Before you hear each item, you will have one minute to study the question.** You will hear each item twice, with an interval of one minute between playings. You will then have time to answer the questions before hearing the next item. Write your answers clearly, in **English**, in the spaces provided.

SECTION 2 — WRITING — 10 marks.

Write your answer clearly, in **French**, in the space provided.

Attempt ALL questions. You may use a French dictionary.

Additional space for answers is provided at the end of this booklet. If you use this space you must clearly identify the question number you are attempting.

You are not allowed to leave the examination room until the end of the test.

Use **blue** or **black** ink.

Before leaving the examination room you must give this booklet to the Invigilator; if you do not, you may lose all the marks for this paper.

MARKS | DO NOT WRITE IN THIS MARGIN

SECTION 1 — LISTENING — 20 marks
Attempt ALL questions

Item 1

Listen to this item about work placements in France.

(a) In what ways can work experience benefit a young person? State any **two** things.

2

_____

_____

(b) The reality of a job is often different. What kind of problems could you experience? State any **two** things.

2

_____

_____

(c)　(i)　What is the main benefit for the company?

1

_____

_____

　　(ii)　What else can a young person bring to the company? State **two** things.

2

_____

_____

(d) Consider the report as a whole. Overall which statement best describes the report? Tick (✓) the correct statement.

1

	Tick (✓)
Work placements benefit an employer most	
Work placements benefit young people most	
Work placements benefit both employers and young people	

MARKS | DO NOT WRITE IN THIS MARGIN

Item 2

Carine and Pierre are discussing future plans.

(a) (i) What is Carine going to do first and why?   **2**

_____

_____

 (ii) What exactly will she do during this year?   **2**

_____

_____

(b) (i) What are Carine's long term plans? State **two** things.   **2**

_____

_____

 (ii) Why does she not want to go to university immediately? State any **two** things.   **2**

_____

_____

(c) In what ways did Carine benefit from working in hotels? State any **two** things.   **2**

_____

_____

(d) According to Carine what will be the positive aspects of her future career?   **2**

_____

_____

[Turn over

SECTION 2 — WRITING — 10 marks

Carine nous a parlé de ce qu'elle veut faire à l'avenir. Quelle sorte de métier est-ce que vous voulez faire à l'avenir? Quels sont les avantages et les inconvénients de prendre une année sabbatique?

Ecris 120—150 mots en français pour exprimer tes idées.

MARKS | DO NOT WRITE IN THIS MARGIN

ANSWER SPACE FOR SECTION 2 (continued)

[Turn over

MARKS | DO NOT WRITE IN THIS MARGIN

ANSWER SPACE FOR SECTION 2 (continued)

[END OF QUESTION PAPER]

MARKS | DO NOT WRITE IN THIS MARGIN

ADDITIONAL SPACE FOR ANSWERS

MARKS | DO NOT WRITE IN THIS MARGIN

ADDITIONAL SPACE FOR ANSWERS

National Qualifications 2016

X730/76/13

French
Listening Transcript

MONDAY, 16 MAY

11:00 AM – 12:00 NOON

This paper must not be seen by any candidate.

The material overleaf is provided for use in an emergency only (eg the recording or equipment proving faulty) or where permission has been given in advance by SQA for the material to be read to candidates with additional support needs. The material must be read exactly as printed.

Instructions to reader(s):

For each item, read the English **once**, then read the French **twice**, with an interval of 1 minute between the two readings. On completion of the second reading of Item Number One, pause for the length of time indicated in brackets after the item, to allow the candidates to write their answers.

Where special arrangements have been agreed in advance to allow the reading of the material, those sections marked **(f)** should be read by a female speaker and those marked **(m)** by a male; those sections marked **(t)** should be read by the teacher.

(t) Item Number One

Listen to this item about work placements in France.

You now have one minute to study the questions for Item Number One.

(f) Si vous voulez faire un stage en France il faut faire des recherches sur internet ou dans des magazines. Mais quels en sont les avantages pour les jeunes?

En effet, un stage peut avoir une grande importance pour tout le monde. Tout d'abord il vous permet de montrer aux futurs employeurs que vous avez non seulement de l'expérience dans le monde du travail mais aussi des compétences utiles pour votre carrière professionnelle. Enfin le stage peut vous permettre également de confirmer (ou non) votre intérêt pour une profession en particulier.

La réalité est souvent très différente. Par exemple on rencontre d'autres problèmes. Quelquefois on ne s'entend pas bien avec le patron. On doit commencer de bonne heure et parfois travailler de longues heures. L'avantage principal pour l'entreprise est que le stagiaire est moins payé qu'un employé permanent. De plus, un stagiaire peut partager de nouvelles idées ainsi que son enthousiasme avec ses collègues.

En conclusion on peut dire que le stage possède des avantages aussi bien pour l'étudiant que pour l'entreprise.

(2 minutes)

(t) **Item Number Two**

Carine and Pierre are discussing future plans.

You now have one minute to study the questions for Item Number Two.

(m) Au lycée on parle beaucoup de ce qu'on va faire à l'avenir. Tu as déjà pensé à ce que tu vas faire? Tu as des projets?

(f) Eh bien, en ce moment je ne sais pas exactement ce que je veux faire. Alors tout d'abord je crois que je vais prendre une année sabbatique. Je suis trop jeune pour choisir une carrière pour la vie.

(m) Alors, qu'est-ce que tu vas faire exactement pendant cette année?

(f) Je vais voyager autour du monde et en profiter pour découvrir de nouvelles cultures. De cette façon j'aurai quelque chose d'intéressant à dire quand je vais chercher un emploi plus tard.

(m) Qu'est-ce que tu as l'intention de faire après ton année sabbatique?

(f) A long terme, j'ai l'intention de travailler avec les enfants. Je vais peut-être faire des études pour devenir institutrice. C'est un métier qui m'attire parce que chaque jour est différent.

(m) Tu ne veux pas aller tout de suite à l'université?

(f) Non, je ne veux pas aller à la fac tout de suite. J'ai peur de faire un mauvais choix et je veux gagner un peu d'argent pour mettre de côté aussi. Comme ça j'aurai encore du temps pour décider quelles études je veux faire.

(m) Quelle sorte de travail est-ce que tu veux faire pendant ton année sabbatique?

(f) Ben, je n'en suis pas sûre. J'ai déjà travaillé comme serveuse et réceptionniste dans un hôtel près de chez moi. Je me suis très bien entendue avec mes collègues et en plus j'ai eu beaucoup de pourboires. A mon avis ce sont des boulots où l'on rencontre beaucoup de monde. J'aime beaucoup le contact avec le public.

(m) Ce n'était pas trop fatigant?

(f) Au contraire. J'ai trouvé que travailler à l'hôtel était un changement complet de ce que je devais faire au lycée. Là je pouvais oublier tout le stress du lycée et en même temps gagner de l'argent en m'amusant.

(m) Mais tu veux être institutrice? Travailler dans une école est dur quand même.

(f) Oui, je le sais, mais on a la satisfaction de voir les élèves faire des progrès. On a la responsabilité de l'avenir de ces jeunes personnes après tout.

(m) Oui, alors là tu as raison.

(t) **End of recording.**

[END OF TRANSCRIPT]

[BLANK PAGE]

DO NOT WRITE ON THIS PAGE

HIGHER

2017

National
Qualifications
2017

X730/76/11

French
Reading

MONDAY, 15 MAY
9:00 AM – 10:40 AM

Total marks — 30

Attempt ALL questions.

Write your answers clearly, in **English**, in the Reading answer booklet provided. In the answer booklet you must clearly identify the question number you are attempting.

You may use a French dictionary.

Use **blue** or **black** ink.

There is a separate question and answer booklet for Directed Writing. You must complete your answer for Directed Writing in the question and answer booklet for Directed Writing.

Before leaving the examination room you must give your Reading answer booklet and your Directed Writing question and answer booklet to the Invigilator; if you do not, you may lose all the marks for this paper.

Total marks — 30

Attempt ALL questions

Read the whole article carefully and then answer, in **English**, ALL the questions that follow.

The article discusses the importance of the media in France.

Les Français et les médias

En France, les médias jouent un rôle très important dans la vie quotidienne. Les Français écoutent la radio, lisent les journaux et regardent la télé. En effet, la télévision représente le premier loisir des Français qui avouent consacrer trois heures au minimum par jour au petit écran, c'est-à-dire cinquante minutes de plus que surfer sur Internet. La télévision reste
5 allumée même si personne ne la regarde! Les films, journaux télévisés et documentaires sont leurs programmes favoris.

Mais ce qui est inquiétant c'est que les programmes sont de moins bonne qualité et c'est pour ça que certains Français parlent de la «télé-réalité». Néanmoins ce genre d'émissions attire beaucoup de téléspectateurs. Jean-Marc, 20 ans, explique: «Après une longue journée
10 je veux tout simplement m'installer dans un fauteuil devant la télé pour m'éloigner du stress du travail. Voilà pourquoi je regarde beaucoup de télé-réalité. Pourtant je reconnais qu'il faut faire attention parce que ces émissions ne respectent pas la vie privée des gens et en plus elles n'ont rien à voir avec la vie du Français moyen.»

Par contre, il ne faut pas oublier que la télévision est un moyen efficace de s'informer de ce
15 qui se passe dans le monde. En seulement trente minutes les Français peuvent s'informer des événements importants dans le monde, tout en mangeant le repas du soir. Ils trouvent les actualités télévisées plus crédibles que les reportages dans la presse populaire. Les aspects positifs sont que les actualités télévisées sont très bien commentées et analysées. Les informations qui intéressent les Français concernent aussi bien les grands débats politiques à
20 l'approche des élections que les catastrophes naturelles même avec ses images brutales et effrayantes.

Les médias traditionnels menacés par Internet?

De nos jours, on a accès aux actualités à n'importe quelle heure de la journée. Les journaux et les magazines français sont moins menacés par Internet parce qu'ils possèdent maintenant
25 aussi leur propre site web. Ce sont surtout les jeunes qui ont tendance à accéder aux médias en ligne, et n'importe où. <u>Juliette Morelle qui prend le train tous les jours observe «On voit les jeunes partout taper sur leur tablette tout en regardant les émissions d'hier soir qu'ils ont téléchargées. Je dois dire que le bruit incessant m'énerve énormément.»</u> Toutefois un grand nombre de Français plus âgés continuent d'acheter leur journal quotidien dans les kiosques
30 ou bien même dans les supermarchés. Chose étonnante, la presse régionale reste le premier média national avec plus de 20 millions de lecteurs parce qu'elle s'intéresse, comme ses lecteurs, plus particulièrement aux événements du quartier. En outre, la presse gratuite est arrivée en 2002 et sa popularité continue d'augmenter et de rivaliser avec la presse payante.

La presse people

35 Soit en ligne, soit sur papier, le public reste fasciné par la vie des personnes célèbres. On voit tous les jours des articles qui racontent les moindres détails de la vie des stars. Les journalistes n'hésitent pas à publier des photos sans permission ni de raconter ce qu'ils mangent au petit déjeuner, avec qui ils sont sortis la semaine dernière. Mais il faut se demander à quoi ça sert et pourquoi les Français ont besoin de lire ce genre d'histoire.
40 Comme la télé-réalité, est-ce seulement un autre moyen d'échapper à la vie quotidienne?

MARKS

Questions

Re-read lines 1—13.

1. Television is the most popular form of media in France. In what ways does the writer highlight this?

3

2. People are watching more and more reality TV.

    (a) What is worrying about this trend?

1

    (b) Why is Jean-Marc attracted to this type of programme?

1

    (c) Which **two** negative aspects does Jean-Marc highlight in relation to these programmes?

2

Re-read lines 14—21.

3. Television news programmes are highly regarded in France.

    (a) In what ways are these programmes convenient for people?

2

    (b) What are the positive aspects of this type of programme?

1

    (c) What type of news reports are French people interested in? Give details.

2

Re-read lines 22—33.

4. The writer goes on to talk about the impact of the Internet on the media. Why are newspapers and magazines less threatened by the Internet?

1

5. According to the article, in what way do many older people access the news?

1

6. Why do regional newspapers still attract more than 20 million readers?

1

Re-read lines 34—40.

7. According to the article, celebrity magazines focus on the smallest details of celebrities' lives. What else does it say about these magazines?

3

MARKS

Questions (continued)

8. Now consider the article as a whole.

    The article discusses how French people access and use the media. Does the writer think that the media play an important role in people's lives? Give reasons for your answer with reference to the text.

    2

9. Translate into English:

    "Juliette Morelle . . . énormément.»" (lines 26 to 28)

    10

[END OF QUESTION PAPER]

[OPEN OUT]

DO NOT WRITE ON THIS PAGE

[BLANK PAGE]

DO NOT WRITE ON THIS PAGE

H

National
Qualifications
2017

Mark

X730/76/02

**French
Directed Writing**

MONDAY, 15 MAY

9:00 AM – 10:40 AM

Fill in these boxes and read what is printed below.

Full name of centre

Town

Forename(s)

Surname

Number of seat

Date of birth

Day   Month   Year

Scottish candidate number

Total marks — 10

Choose ONE scenario on *Page two* and write your answer clearly, in **French**, in the space provided in this booklet. You must clearly identify the scenario number you are attempting.

You may use a French dictionary.

Additional space for answers is provided at the end of this booklet.

Use **blue** or **black** ink.

There is a separate answer booklet for Reading. You must complete your answers for Reading in the answer booklet for Reading.

Before leaving the examination room you must give this Directed Writing question and answer booklet and your Reading answer booklet to the Invigilator; if you do not, you may lose all the marks for this paper.

MARKS | DO NOT WRITE IN THIS MARGIN

Total marks — 10

Choose **one** of the following two scenarios.

SCENARIO 1: Learning

> You recently took part in an exchange with your partner school in France. On your return you were asked to write an account **in French** of your experience for your school/college website.

You must include the following information and **you should try to add** other relevant details:

- where the school was located **and** what you thought of the school
- what you did to improve your French during your stay
- what benefits you gained from taking part in the school exchange
- whether or not you would recommend participating in a school exchange

You should write approximately 120—150 words.

OR

SCENARIO 2: Employability

> Last year you spent a month working in France. On your return you were asked to write an account **in French** of your experience for your school/college website.

You must include the following information and **you should try to add** other relevant details:

- who you went with **and** how you travelled
- what you had to do in your job
- what you did with the money you earned
- how your experience will benefit your future career

You should write approximately 120—150 words.

MARKS | DO NOT WRITE IN THIS MARGIN

ANSWER SPACE

Scenario number

[Turn over

MARKS | DO NOT WRITE IN THIS MARGIN

ANSWER SPACE (continued)

MARKS | DO NOT WRITE IN THIS MARGIN

ANSWER SPACE (continued)

MARKS DO NOT WRITE IN THIS MARGIN

ANSWER SPACE (continued)

[END OF QUESTION PAPER]

MARKS | DO NOT WRITE IN THIS MARGIN

ADDITIONAL SPACE FOR ANSWERS

MARKS DO NOT WRITE IN THIS MARGIN

ADDITIONAL SPACE FOR ANSWERS

H

National Qualifications 2017

Mark

X730/76/03

French
Listening and Writing

MONDAY, 15 MAY

11:00 AM – 12:00 NOON

Fill in these boxes and read what is printed below.

Full name of centre

Town

Forename(s)

Surname

Number of seat

Date of birth

Day	Month	Year

Scottish candidate number

Total marks — 30

SECTION 1 — LISTENING — 20 marks

You will hear two items in French. **Before you hear each item, you will have one minute to study the questions.** You will hear each item twice, with an interval of one minute between playings. You will then have time to answer the questions before hearing the next item. Write your answers clearly, in **English**, in the spaces provided.

SECTION 2 — WRITING — 10 marks

Write your answer clearly, in **French**, in the space provided.

You may use a French dictionary.

Additional space for answers is provided at the end of this booklet. If you use this space you must clearly identify the question number you are attempting.

Use **blue** or **black** ink.

You are not allowed to leave the examination room until the end of the test.

Before leaving the examination room you must give this booklet to the Invigilator; if you do not, you may lose all the marks for this paper.

MARKS | DO NOT WRITE IN THIS MARGIN

SECTION 1 — LISTENING — 20 marks

Attempt ALL questions

Item 1

You hear a radio report about holidays.

(a) What reasons do young people give for **not** wanting to spend holidays with their parents? State any **two**.

2

_____

_____

(b) It is normal for teenagers to want their independence. They also need their freedom. What else is important to them at this age? State **two** things.

2

_____

_____

(c) (i) Some parents are protective. What types of holidays are more suitable for their children? State any **one** thing.

1

_____

(ii) Give **one** example of how young people can benefit from these holidays.

1

_____

(d) Give **two** reasons why young people continue to go on holiday with their parents.

2

_____

_____

Item 2

Pauline talks about her experience at a colonie de vacances, a summer camp for young people.

(a) Pauline first went to a colonie de vacances when she was 8 years old. Why did her parents send her there? State **two** things.

2

_____

_____

(b) (i) What type of activities did she do at the colonie de vacances? State **two** things.

2

_____

_____

   (ii) What was the aim of these activities? State any **one** thing.

1

_____

(c) Pauline grew in confidence at the colonie de vacances. What example does she give of this? State **two** things.

2

_____

_____

(d) She goes on to talk about a boy of the same age that she remembers.

   (i) He was very shy. What problems did the boy have? Give any **one** example.

1

_____

   (ii) What did Pauline do to help the boy? Give any **one** example.

1

_____

(e) Pauline is now working in a colonie de vacances. What does her job involve? State **two** things.

2

_____

_____

(f) This year she is going to a colonie de vacances near the Spanish border. Why will this be a good experience for her? State any **one** thing.

1

_____

MARKS | DO NOT WRITE IN THIS MARGIN

SECTION 2 — WRITING — 10 marks

Pauline nous a parlé de son expérience dans une colonie de vacances. Et toi, tu aimes les vacances organisées comme Pauline ou préfères-tu partir avec tes copains ou tes parents?

Ecris 120—150 mots en français pour exprimer tes idées.

ANSWER SPACE FOR SECTION 2 (continued)

MARKS | DO NOT WRITE IN THIS MARGIN

ANSWER SPACE FOR SECTION 2 (continued)

Page six

[END OF QUESTION PAPER]

MARKS | DO NOT WRITE IN THIS MARGIN

ADDITIONAL SPACE FOR ANSWERS

ADDITIONAL SPACE FOR ANSWERS

National Qualifications 2017

X730/76/13

French
Listening Transcript

MONDAY, 15 MAY

11:00 AM – 12:00 NOON

This paper must not be seen by any candidate.

The material overleaf is provided for use in an emergency only (eg the recording or equipment proving faulty) or where permission has been given in advance by SQA for the material to be read to candidates with additional support needs. The material must be read exactly as printed.

Instructions to reader(s):

For each item, read the English **once**, then read the French **twice**, with an interval of 1 minute between the two readings. On completion of the second reading of Item Number One, pause for the length of time indicated in brackets after the item, to allow the candidates to write their answers.

Where special arrangements have been agreed in advance to allow the reading of the material, those sections marked **(f)** should be read by a female speaker and those marked **(m)** by a male; those sections marked **(t)** should be read by the teacher.

(t) Item Number One

You hear a radio report about holidays.

You now have one minute to study the questions for Item Number One.

(f) Pour beaucoup de familles, les vacances représentent le soleil, le repos, les loisirs. Mais, elles peuvent être aussi une source de disputes entre les parents et les adolescents. Les adolescents disent souvent «je ne suis plus un bébé», «les vacances en famille c'est ennuyeux», «mes copains me manquent».

Pour un adolescent il est normal de vouloir son indépendance. A cet âge, il a besoin de liberté, de prendre ses propres décisions, et de faire ses propres erreurs.

Si les parents sont protecteurs et inquiets, ils ne sont pas capables de laisser leur enfant partir tout seul avec ses copains. Ils préfèrent les vacances organisées, par exemple des séjours linguistiques ou des séjours en famille. Ce sont des options qui permettent aux jeunes de perfectionner une langue ou de découvrir une autre culture. S'il y a un problème il y a toujours un adulte à proximité.

Malgré tout cela, les jeunes aiment toujours partir en vacances avec les parents parce qu'ils se sentent en sécurité et en plus les parents paient tout: la nourriture, le logement et les activités. Finalement, partir en vacances en famille, ce n'est pas si mal après tout!

(2 minutes)

(t) Item Number Two

Pauline talks about her experience at a colonie de vacances, a summer camp for young people.

You now have one minute to study the questions for Item Number Two.

(m) Pauline, tu peux me parler de ton premier séjour en colonie de vacances?

(f) Mon premier séjour dans une colonie de vacances était à l'âge de huit ans. J'étais un enfant très actif et j'aimais beaucoup être en plein air. Comme j'étais fille unique, je n'avais pas de frère et sœur pour jouer avec moi. Alors mes parents ont décidé de m'envoyer en colonie de vacances. Comme ça, j'étais moins seule.

(m) Quelles sortes d'activités est-ce que tu as fait?

(f) Pendant mon premier séjour j'ai fait beaucoup de choses, j'ai fait de la peinture et le soir j'ai joué à des jeux de société avec les autres enfants. Le but de ces activités était d'apprendre à jouer ensemble et à travailler en équipe.

(m) Qu'est-ce que tu as appris en tant qu'enfant en colonie de vacances?

(f) J'ai appris à être plus indépendante, et je trouve que je suis maintenant plus mûre. En plus, j'ai plus confiance en moi — par exemple j'ai aidé les plus jeunes quand ils avaient des problèmes, quand ils avaient le mal du pays ou quand leurs parents leur manquaient.

(m) Tu te souviens d'une personne en particulier?

(f) Oui, je me souviens d'un garçon du même âge que moi qui était très timide. Il ne parlait pas beaucoup et il ne voulait pas participer aux activités. J'ai passé beaucoup de temps avec lui, on a beaucoup parlé. Après trois ou quatre jours il est devenu moins réservé, plus bavard, plus sociable. A la fin des vacances il ne voulait pas rentrer chez lui. Cette expérience m'a encouragé à devenir animatrice moi-même.

(m) Alors, maintenant que tu es animatrice dans une colonie de vacances, qu'est-ce que tu fais exactement comme travail?

(f) Tous les soirs, il y a une réunion avec les collègues où l'on parle de l'emploi du temps pour le lendemain. Je dois aussi surveiller les enfants aux heures de repas.

(m) Où vas-tu travailler cette année?

(f) Pour la première fois je vais dans le sud de la France près de la frontière espagnole. C'est une région que je ne connais pas du tout. Alors, ce sera une bonne expérience pour moi. Et puisque cette année j'ai appris l'espagnol j'espère que je pourrai aller en Espagne pendant mes vacances.

(m) Tu as de la chance Pauline. Amuse-toi bien!

(f) Merci bien.

(t) End of recording.

[END OF TRANSCRIPT]

[BLANK PAGE]

DO NOT WRITE ON THIS PAGE

HIGHER FRENCH
2015

Reading

Question		Expected response(s)
1.	(a)	• An object of prestige <u>and</u> social status/ standing/status symbol • Something (which they use) to define their personality
	(b)	• <u>1 in 20</u> develop/show symptoms of addiction/dependency **OR** • Some people take/use <u>it into/under the shower</u> *Any one of above 2 points for 1 mark*
	(c)	• They do not get enough sleep/they don't sleep as/so much/they can lose quite a bit of sleep • Their school results/grades are not as/ less good/suffer/school results get worse/ worsen/it lowers their school results • Relationships with parents are (often) strained/tense/stressful • They spend/devote a large/big/good part/ bit of their time/life on/to/with their phone/it *Any two of above 4 points for 2 marks*
2.		• Some feel naked/bare/nude without it • Some say they don't know how to/can't live/ be/exist without it • Some are <u>ashamed/embarrassed</u> if (the/ their) phone/device/machine/handset has become/is (too) old/dated/old-fashioned *Any two of above 3 points for 2 marks*
3.	(a)	• They sleep/have/keep (with) their phone (switched on) under/on/by their <u>pillow</u> • They put their phone <u>on the bedside table/ unit/cabinet</u> (so that it's just beside their bed/so that they can be contacted at any moment)
	(b)	• He uses it every day (without exception) • He goes to bed/falls asleep/sleeps with <u>and</u> gets/wakes up with it • He (has to/must) consult(s)/look(s) at/ check(s) texts/emails/phone <u>all the time/ constantly/always</u> • He could not cope/manage/last/go/survive/ be (for 30 minutes) without his phone *Any three of above 4 points for 3 marks*
4.		• Can communicate with several/a lot of/lots of many/more people/more than one person <u>at the same time/at once</u> • They have become/are <u>more</u> private <u>than</u> phone call(s) • They can (even) send (a) text(s)/text <u>in the cinema</u> (discreetly)
5.	(a)	• Text messaging/it is destroying young people's ability/capacity to express themselves <u>when they write/in writing/</u> Young people cannot express themselves <u>when they write/in writing</u> **OR** Pupils (have a tendency to) neglect/pay less attention to their grammar • It is reflected/seen/shows (a lot) in their studies/work
	(b)	• He sends <u>about/more than/over/nearly a hundred</u> texts <u>a day</u> **OR** • He can text while doing something else (at the same time) *Any one of above 2 points for 1 mark*
6.		*Possible answers:* Negative: • Can't live without mobile phones (in shower/ under pillow/texting in cinema) • Adverse effect on school work and results • Affects their sleep • Relationships with parents Positive: • Useful in school and work • Communicates with lots of people at the same time Neutral: With back up

Question 7 – Translation

The translation into English is allocated 10 marks. The text for translation will be divided into a number of sense units. Each sense unit is worth 2 marks, which will be awarded according to the quality and accuracy of the translation into English.

1	2 marks available:
La plupart des ados considèrent leur portable comme leur meilleur ami.	**Most teenagers consider their mobile phone to be their best friend.**
La plupart	The majority of/most
des ados	teenagers/teens/young people/adolescents
considèrent leur portable	consider/think of/regard their mobile(s)/phone(s)
comme leur meilleur ami.	to be (like)/as their best friend.

2	2 marks available:
Les portables sont souvent équipés de fonctions ultra-performantes.	**Phones are often equipped with high performing functions/features.**
Les portables sont souvent équipés de	(the/their) mobiles are often equipped/fitted/come with
fonctions ultra-performantes.	ultra/high/highly performing functions ultra/highly-efficient functions.

3	*2 marks available:*
Ils permettent aux jeunes non seulement d'envoyer des textos,	**They allow young people not only to send texts/to not only send texts,**
Ils permettent	They permit/let
aux jeunes	youngsters/young folk(s)
non seulement	not only
d' envoyer des textos,	to text/to send text messages,

4	*2 marks available:*
mais aussi de télécharger de la musique achetée en ligne	**but (also) (to) download music bought/purchased on-line/on the internet**
mais aussi de	but also to
télécharger de la musique	download the music
achetée en ligne	that they buy/have bought/ (have) purchase(d) online

5	*2 marks available:*
et, dans une moindre mesure de jouer à des jeux préinstallés.	**and, to a lesser extent, to play preloaded/ preinstalled games.**
et, dans une moindre mesure	on a lesser/smaller scale
de jouer	(to) play
à des jeux préinstallés.	already loaded/installed.

Directed Writing

Candidates will write a piece of extended writing in French addressing a scenario that has four related bullet points. Candidates must address each bullet point. The first bullet point contains two pieces of information to be addressed. The remaining three bullet points contain one piece of information each. There is a choice of two scenarios and learners must choose one of these.

Mark	Content	Accuracy	Language resource: variety, range, structures
10	• The content is comprehensive • All bullet points are addressed fully and some candidates may also provide additional relevant information	• The language is accurate in all four bullets. However, where the candidate attempts to go beyond the range of the task, a slightly higher number of inaccuracies need not detract from the overall very good impression • A comprehensive range of verbs is used accurately and tenses are consistent and accurate • There is evidence of confident handling of all aspects of grammar and accurate spelling, although the language may contain a number of minor errors, or even one serious error • Where the candidate attempts to go beyond the range of the task, a slightly higher number of inaccuracies need not detract from the overall very good impression	• The language used is detailed and complex • There is good use of adjectives, adverbs, prepositional phrases and, where appropriate, word order • A comprehensive range of verbs/verb forms, tenses and constructions is used • Some modal verbs and infinitives may be used • The candidate is comfortable with the first person of the verb and generally uses a different verb in each sentence • Sentences are mainly complex and accurate • The language flows well

Mark	Content	Accuracy	Language resource: variety, range, structures
8	• The content is clear • All bullet points are addressed clearly. The response to one bullet point may be thin, although other bullet points are dealt with in some detail	• The language is mostly accurate. Where the candidate attempts to use detailed and complex language, this may be less successful, although basic structures are used accurately • A range of verbs is used accurately and tenses are generally consistent and accurate • There may be a few errors in spelling, adjective endings and, where relevant, case endings. Use of accents is less secure, where relevant	• The language used is detailed and complex • In one bullet point the language may be more basic than might otherwise be expected at this level • The candidate uses a range of verbs/verb forms and other constructions • There may be less variety in the verbs used • The candidate is comfortable with the first person of the verb and generally uses a different verb in each sentence • Sentences are generally complex and mainly accurate • Overall the writing will be very competent, essentially correct, but may be pedestrian
6	• The content is adequate and may be similar to that of an 8 • Bullet points may be addressed adequately, however one of the bullet points may not be addressed	• The language may be mostly accurate in two or three bullet points. However, in the remaining one or two, control of the language structure may deteriorate significantly • The verbs are generally correct, but basic • Tenses may be inconsistent, with present tenses being used at times instead of past tenses • There may be errors in spelling, adjective endings and some prepositions may be inaccurate or omitted. There are quite a few errors in other parts of speech – personal pronouns, gender of nouns, adjective endings, cases (where relevant), singular/plural confusion – and in the use of accents (where relevant) • Overall, there is more correct than incorrect and there is the impression that the candidate can handle tenses	• There are some examples of detailed and complex language • The language is perhaps repetitive and uses a limited range of verbs and fixed phrases not appropriate to this level • The candidate relies on a limited range of vocabulary and structures • There is minimal use of adjectives, probably mainly after "is" • The candidate has a limited knowledge of plurals • A limited range of verbs is used to address some of the bullet points • The candidate copes with the past tense of some verbs • When using the perfect tense, the past participle is incorrect or the auxiliary verb is omitted on occasion • Sentences are mainly single clause and may be brief
4	• The content may be limited and the Directed Writing may be presented as a single paragraph • Bullet points may be addressed in a limited way or • **Two** of the bullet points are not be addressed	• The language is mainly inaccurate and after the first bullet the control of the language structure may deteriorate significantly • A limited range of verbs is used • Ability to form tenses is inconsistent • In the use of the perfect tense the auxiliary verb is omitted on a number of occasions • There may be confusion between the singular and plural form of verbs • There are errors in many other parts of speech – gender of nouns, cases, singular/plural confusion – and in spelling and, where appropriate, word order • Several errors are serious, perhaps showing mother tongue interference	• There is limited use of detailed and complex language • The language is repetitive, with undue reliance on fixed phrases and a limited range of common basic verbs such as to be, to have, to play, to watch • The candidate mainly copes only with simple language • The verbs "was" and "went" may also be used correctly • Sentences are basic and there may be one sentence that is not intelligible to a sympathetic native speaker • An English word may appear in the writing or a word may be omitted • There may be an example of serious dictionary misuse

Mark	Content	Accuracy	Language resource: variety, range, structures
2	• The content may be basic or similar to that of a 4 or even a 6 • Bullet points are addressed with difficulty	• The language is inaccurate in all four bullets and there is little control of language structure • Many of the verbs are incorrect or even omitted. There is little evidence of tense control • There are many errors in other parts of speech — personal pronouns, gender of nouns, cases, singular/plural confusion, prepositions, for instance	• There is little use, if any, of detailed and complex language • Verbs used more than once may be written differently on each occasion • The candidate displays almost no knowledge of the past tense of verbs • The candidate cannot cope with more than one or two basic verbs • Sentences are very short and some sentences may not be understood by a sympathetic native speaker
0	• The content is very basic • The candidate is unable to address the bullet points Or • **Three** or more of the bullet points are not addressed	• The language is seriously inaccurate in all four bullets and there is almost no control of language structure • Most errors are serious • Virtually nothing is correct • Very little is intelligible to a sympathetic native speaker	• There is no evidence of detailed and complex language • The candidate may only cope with the verbs to have and to be • There may be several examples of mother tongue interference • English words are used • Very few words are written correctly in the modern language • There may be several examples of serious dictionary misuse

Section 1 — Listening

Item 1

Question		Expected response(s)
(a)	(i)	• Encourages you to take (more) responsibility/gives you (more) responsibility/gives a sense of responsibility/ you learn more responsibility/teaches you responsibility
	(ii)	• Film dialogues/conversations • Download language/linguistic games/ activities • Exchanging emails with/send emails to penpal(s) abroad/foreign correspondent(s)/ penpal(s) in other countries/talk to correspondent(s) abroad via email *Any two of above 3 points for 2 marks*
(b)		• It encourages them to work as a team • It is good for pupils who are competitive/like to win/competitive pupils benefit from this
(c)		• They live in the North East of France • The journey/voyage/trip was not (too) long/ was short **and** not (too) expensive/was cheap *Need both parts for 1 mark*
(d)		• Valérie is positive about the use of technology in language classes (middle box)

Item 2

Question		Expected response(s)
(a)		• (Lots of) Italian speaking pupils/students in her school
(b)		• It is (very) easy to go to Italy or visit Italy • Nearest Italian town 50 kilometres away • Opportunity to improve language by chatting/talking (to people) in cafés/markets *Any two of above 3 points for 2 marks*
(c)	(i)	• In her third year of university
	(ii)	• (Earn/gain) money
(d)		• Contact companies/a company (during the second year at university) • Some teachers/professors (at university) have a list of companies (which take students) • Organise/sort transport and accommodation/ places to stay/places to live • Research on the internet *Any three of above 4 points for 3 marks*
(e)		• (Going to) work/find a job as soon as possible • Find an interesting job/work/job she is interested in • Use her language in (the world of) business/ commerce/trade *Any two of above 3 points for 2 marks*
(f)		• Broaden/widen/enlarge/expand your horizons **OR** • Essential/useful/indispensable in (the world of) business/trade **and** tourism/in the business **and** tourist industries *Any one of above 2 points for 1 mark*
(g)		• Take part in/contribute to conferences/ meetings **OR** • Use your language skills to travel (the world) *Any one of above 2 points for 1 mark*

Section 2 — Writing

Candidates will write 120–150 words in a piece of extended writing in French addressing a stimulus of three questions in French.

Mark	Content	Accuracy	Language resource: variety, range, structures
10	• The content is comprehensive • The topic is addressed fully, in a balanced way • Some candidates may also provide additional information • Overall this comes over as a competent, well thought-out response to the task which reads naturally	• The language is accurate throughout. However where the candidate attempts to go beyond the range of the task, a slightly higher number of inaccuracies need not detract from the overall very good impression • A comprehensive range of verbs is used accurately and tenses are consistent and accurate • There is evidence of confident handling of all aspects of grammar and spelling accurately, although the language may contain a number of minor errors, or even one serious major error	• The language used is detailed and complex • There is good use of adjectives, adverbs, prepositional phrases and, where appropriate, word order • A comprehensive range of verbs/verb forms, tenses and constructions is used • Some modal verbs and infinitives may be used • The candidate is comfortable with the first person of the verb and generally uses a different verb in each sentence • The candidate uses co-ordinating conjunctions and subordinate clauses throughout the writing • Sentences are mainly complex and accurate • The language flows well
8	• The content is clear • The topic is addressed clearly	• The language is mostly accurate. However where the candidate attempts to use detailed and complex language, this may be less successful, although basic structures are used accurately • A range of verbs is used accurately and tenses are generally consistent and accurate • There may be a few errors in spelling, adjective endings and, where relevant, case endings. Use of accents is less secure • Verbs and other parts of speech are used accurately but simply	• The language used is detailed and complex • The candidate uses a range of verbs/verb forms and other constructions • There may be less variety in the verbs used • The candidate is comfortable with the first person of the verb and generally uses a different verb in each sentence • Most of the more complex sentences use co-ordinating conjunctions, and there may also be examples of subordinating conjunctions where appropriate • Sentences are generally complex and mainly accurate • At times the language may be more basic than might otherwise be expected at this level • There may be an example of minor misuse of dictionary • Overall the writing will be very competent, essentially correct, but may be pedestrian

Mark	Content	Accuracy	Language resource: variety, range, structures
6	• The content is adequate and may be similar to that of an 8 or a 10 • The topic is addressed adequately	• The language may be mostly accurate. However, in places, control of the language structure may deteriorate significantly • The verbs are generally correct, but basic. Tenses may be inconsistent, with present tenses being used at times instead of past tenses • There may be errors in spelling, e.g. reversal of vowel combinations adjective endings and some prepositions may be inaccurate or omitted, e.g. I went the town. There are quite a few errors in other parts of speech – personal pronouns, gender of nouns, adjective endings, cases, singular/plural confusion – and in the use of accents • Overall, there is more correct than incorrect and there is the impression that the candidate can handle tenses	• There are some examples of detailed and complex language • The language is perhaps repetitive and uses a limited range of verbs and fixed phrases not appropriate to this level • The candidate relies on a limited range of vocabulary and structures • There is minimal use of adjectives, probably mainly after "is" • The candidate has a limited knowledge of plurals • The candidate copes with the present tense of most verbs • Where the candidate attempts constructions with modal verbs, these are not always successful • Sentences are mainly single clause and may be brief • There may be some misuse of dictionary
4	• The content may be limited and may be presented as a single paragraph • The topic is addressed in a limited way	• The language used to address the more predictable aspects of the task may be accurate. However, major errors occur when the candidate attempts to address a less predictable aspect • A limited range of verbs is used • Ability to form tenses is inconsistent • In the use of the perfect tense the auxiliary verb is omitted on a number of occasions • There may be confusion between the singular and plural form of verbs • There are errors in many other parts of speech – gender of nouns, cases, singular/plural confusion – and in spelling and, where appropriate, word order • Several errors are serious, perhaps showing mother tongue interference • Overall there is more incorrect than correct	• There is limited use of detailed and complex language and the language is mainly simple and predictable • The language is repetitive, with undue reliance on fixed phrases and a limited range of common basic verbs such as to be, to have, to play, to watch • There is inconsistency in the use of various expressions, especially verbs • Sentences are basic and there may be one sentence that is not intelligible to a sympathetic native speaker • An English word may appear in the writing or a word may be omitted • There may be an example of serious dictionary misuse

Mark	Content	Accuracy	Language resource: variety, range, structures
2	• The content may be basic or similar to that of a 4 or even a 6 • The topic is thinly addressed	• The language is almost completely inaccurate throughout the writing and there is little control of language structure • Many of the verbs are incorrect or even omitted. There is little evidence of tense control • There are many errors in other parts of speech — personal pronouns, gender of nouns, cases, singular/plural confusion • Prepositions are not used correctly	• There is little use, if any, of detailed and complex language • The candidate has a very limited vocabulary • Verbs used more than once may be written differently on each occasion • The candidate cannot cope with more than one or two basic verbs • Sentences are very short and some sentences may not be understood by a sympathetic native speaker • Several English or "made-up" words may appear in the writing • There are examples of serious dictionary misuse
0	• The content is very basic • The candidate is unable to address the topic	• The language is seriously inaccurate throughout the writing and there is almost no control of language structure • (Virtually) nothing is correct • Most of the errors are serious • Very little is intelligible to a sympathetic native speaker	• There is no evidence of detailed and complex language • The candidate copes only with "have" and "am" • There may be several examples of mother tongue interference • Very few words are written correctly in the modern language • English words are used • There may be several examples of serious dictionary misuse

HIGHER FRENCH 2016

Reading

Question			Expected response(s)
1.			• She grew up far from New York/in (the state of) Kentucky • She did sport(s) with her (older) brother(s), <u>while being a cheerleader/majorette</u> • She has never/not taken drama/acting/theatre class(es)/lesson(s)/course(s) • Neither of her parents/her parents don't work in (the) (world of) cinema/film industry *Any three of above 4 points for 3 marks*
2.	(a)		• (Almost) <u>every/each week</u>, dozens/lots of new films with teenage/young lead actors/heroes/main characters/protagonists are released/come out/appear (in the cinema/in cinema)
	(b)		• The (lead) actor(s)/(main) character(s)/protagonist(s)/(typical) hero(es)/they/he/she is/are becoming <u>younger and younger/more and more young</u>
	(c)		• It attracts a (new) <u>young</u> audience/an audience of youth/group(s) of <u>young</u> people/customers/clients/clientele OR • It attracts people who are equally young/of a similar age (to the main characters)/who are also teenagers/cinema goers are becoming younger also *Any one of above 2 points for 1 mark*
3.	(a)		• He/she/it doesn't/they don't respect/follow/disrespect(s) any/the/all of the rules (any more)
	(b)	(i)	• Incapable of giving/setting/making/establishing/putting limits/boundaries/parameters/rules Not able to/can't give/set/make/establish/put limits/boundaries/parameters/rules • (Often) abandon/give up their role/duty/duties (as parents)
		(ii)	• The teenagers/children/kids/they are (often) (left) <u>alone/by themselves at home/in the house/home alone</u>

Question			Expected response(s)
4.	(a)		• Teenagers do not know how to/can't/are unable to communicate with/speak/talk to peers/classmates/friends <u>and/or</u> adults/grown-ups (around them) • They spend/pass <u>all</u> (of) their/the time in front of/on/behind their computer (screen)/laptop
	(b)		• They are/he/she is shown as immature/angry/bad tempered/moody OR • It shows/they show their immaturity/anger/bad temper *Any one of above 2 points for 1 mark*
	(c)		• (Films that feature/show/films with) <u>groups/gangs/crowds/hordes/a lot of</u> young people/teenagers/friends/pals/mates/buddies (together) *plus one of the following* • who are (sometimes) cheeky/insolent/impudent • who muck about/get up to mischief/do silly/stupid things/being silly/stupid • who help <u>one another/each other</u> • try to solve <u>their/each other's</u> problems *Idea of groups plus one additional detail = 2 marks*
5.	(a)		• The <u>daily/everyday</u> life (of young people) OR • Difficult/trying relationship(s)/relations/difficulty(ies) (getting along) with parents/difficultly(ies) between teens and parents *Any one of above 2 points for 1 mark*
	(b)	(i)	• Denouncing/condemning/arguing against/opposing/fighting (against)/showing/portraying/exposing/talking about/reporting on/highlighting war/poverty/inequality *NB: need verb plus one detail for 1 mark*
		(ii)	• They/one/you/we/children/people/teenagers grow up <u>too fast/quickly/soon/early</u> • They/one/you/we/children/people become adult without (ever) experiencing adolescence/being a teenager/teen *Any one of above 2 points for 1 mark*

Question	Expected response(s)
6.	*Assertion + justification in English = 2 marks* Outline of possible response and evidence: Young people are shown negatively/in a bad/pessimistic light/as troubled/as problematic/as stereotypes/as clichés • image of teenager who cannot communicate • who spend all their time in front of a computer • rebellious/disrespect rules • product of poor parenting • isolated/unhappy/alone • any other negative detail from the text OR Young people are shown positively/in a good/optimistic light/as kind/as helpful • groups of friends who help each other solving their problems • interested in world issues/war/poverty/inequality • any other positive detail from the text OR Young people are shown in both a positive and negative/neutral light • any one positive detail and any one negative detail from above OR Young people in western and developing countries are represented differently In Western countries: • difficulties with parents • daily life In developing countries: • teenagers denouncing war/poverty/inequality • they grow up too quickly *NB: any one detail from western countries and one detail from developing countries*

Question 7 – Translation

The translation into English is allocated 10 marks. The text for translation will be divided into a number of sense units. Each sense unit is worth 2 marks, which will be awarded according to the quality and accuracy of the translation into English.

1	*2 marks available:*
Ces films illustrent que les jeunes héros sont partout dans les films.	**These films illustrate/ show that young heroes are everywhere in films.**
Ces films	These/those films/movies
illustrent que	illustrate/show/demonstrate (that/how)
les jeunes héros	young heroes
sont partout dans les films.	are everywhere in films/movies in the films/movies in film.

2	*2 marks available:*
Les directeurs de cinéma se sont inspirés des problèmes des jeunes	**Film directors are inspired by young people's problems**
Les directeurs de cinéma	(The) (film/cinema) directors (The) directors of cinema
se sont inspirés	are inspired by take inspiration from
des problèmes des jeunes	young people's problems the problems of young people the problems young people have/face

3	*2 marks available:*
tels que la drogue, l'amour et le stress des examens.	**such as drugs, love and exam stress.**
tels que	such as like
la drogue, l'amour et le stress des examens.	drugs, love and exam stress/ the stress of exams.

4	*2 marks available:*
Cependant il faut avouer que les adolescents qui se disputent avec des adultes	**However, you have to admit that teenagers arguing with adults**
Cependant	However/but/nevertheless
il faut avouer que	you/one/we have to/must/ need to/got to admit/confess (that) it must be admitted/confessed (that)
les adolescents qui se disputent avec des adultes	teenagers/adolescents arguing/fighting/quarrelling with/who argue/fight/quarrel/ have disputes with adults

5	*2 marks available:*
n'est pas du tout un nouveau thème au cinéma.	**is not at all a new theme in film.**
n'est pas du tout	is not at all is not in any way
un nouveau thème au cinéma.	a new theme in film/(the) cinema/movies/film industry a new cinematic theme.

Directed Writing

Please refer to pages 90–92 for advice on the general marking principles for Higher French — Directing Writing.

Section 1 — Listening

Item 1

Question			Expected response(s)
1.	(a)		• You gain experience of the <u>world of work</u> • You gain/develop/have useful skills/ necessary skills/useful competence • It confirms whether or not you are interested in a particular job/confirms what you would like to do/whether you want to do the job or not (candidate must convey idea of interest in the job) *Any two of above 3 points for 2 marks*
	(b)		• You do not get on with/do not have a good relationship with the <u>manager/boss</u> • You have to start/begin/commence early • You have to work long hours/shifts *NB: start early and finish late = 2 marks* *Any two of above 3 points for 2 marks*
	(c)	(i)	• (The person on work experience) is paid less/isn't paid as much/gets low<u>er</u> wages/ it's cheaper
		(ii)	• New/fresh ideas/perspectives • Enthusiasm/they are enthusiastic
	(d)		• Work placements benefit both employers and young people (last box)

Item 2

Question			Expected response(s)
2.	(a)	(i)	• Take a gap year/a year off/sabbatical year/year abroad • She is (too) <u>young/not old enough</u> to <u>choose/decide</u> on a career for life/future career *NB: there must be the idea of not knowing what career to choose*
		(ii)	• Travel (around) the <u>world</u> • (Benefit from) discovering/seeing/ experiencing new culture(s)
	(b)	(i)	• She wants to work with children • Become a <u>primary</u> teacher *NB: Teach children = 1 mark*
		(ii)	• She is scared of making/she does not want to make a bad/wrong choice/decision • She wants to earn/make/save money (to put aside for university) • She wants (time) to decide which <u>course/ subjects</u> she wants to study/doesn't know which <u>subjects</u> to do/doesn't know what to study *Any two of above 3 points for 2 marks*
	(c)		• She got on well with her <u>colleagues/other staff</u> • She got lots of tips • She could meet lots of people/likes the contact with the public • Complete/total change <u>from school</u> • Forgot/got away from the stress of school • Earned money <u>at the same time</u> as/<u>while</u> having fun/enjoying herself *Any two of above 6 points for 2 marks*
	(d)		• The <u>satisfaction</u> of seeing pupils/children/ students making progress • The fact that she is responsible <u>for their future</u>/plays a part in shaping <u>their future</u>

Section 2 — Writing

Please refer to pages 93–95 for advice on general marking principles for Higher French — Writing.

HIGHER FRENCH
2017

Reading

Question			Expected response(s)
1.			• They <u>watch</u> (television) <u>at least/minimum</u> <u>three</u> hours <u>a day</u> • This is 50 minutes <u>more than</u> surfing the net/going online • The TV is on even if <u>no-one/nobody is/people</u> are not watching it
2.	(a)		• The programmes are of <u>less</u> good <u>quality</u>/less/not <u>as</u> good/low<u>er</u>/poor<u>er</u>/worse quality OR • Programmes have reduced in (good) <u>quality</u> *Any one of above 2 points for 1 mark*
	(b)		• To get away/distance/move away from/escape/detach <u>yourself</u>/remove <u>yourself</u> from the stress of <u>work</u>
	(c)		• They don't respect people's <u>private/personal</u> life/lives OR • Your privacy is not respected • They have nothing to do with/are nothing like the <u>average</u> French <u>person's</u> life/nothing like the lives of an <u>average</u> French <u>person</u>
3.	(a)		• They/it <u>only</u> last(s) 30 minutes/<u>no more than</u> 30 minutes • You can watch them (all)/you can find out what is happening in the world <u>while/when/whilst/at the same time as</u> you are eating your <u>evening meal/dinner/tea</u> *NB: You can find out what is happening in the world in only 30 minutes = 1 mark*
	(b)		• News/it/they is/are <u>very well</u>-presented/commented/commentated/reported/covered <u>and</u> analysed OR • The news has <u>very good</u> commentary/commentaries/comments/coverage <u>and</u> analysis *Any one of above 2 points for 1 mark*
	(c)		• (Big) political debates/discussions in the run up to/approaching/near (the) election(s)/at election time • <u>Natural</u> disasters/catastrophes with brutal/frightening/scary/terrifying pictures/photos/images *NB: Big political debates in the run up to elections <u>rather than</u> natural disasters with brutal images = 1 mark*

Question			Expected response(s)
4.			• They have/own/possess their <u>own</u> websites
5.			• (Older people) <u>continue to/still/keep</u> buy(ing) their <u>daily/everyday</u> newspaper (in kiosks or supermarkets)
6.			• They are interested in <u>local</u> events/events in the <u>area/neighbourhood/district</u>
7.			• They publish/print/release <u>photographs/pictures/images without permission/asking them</u> • They report/share details/publish/print/release/tell/talk about/write about <u>what</u> they eat for <u>breakfast</u> • (They report/share details/publish/print/release/tell/talk about/write) about <u>who</u> they went out with <u>last/previous week/the week before</u>
8.			Yes, it plays an important role because **+ a general reason** eg: • French people access a wide range of media (TV, Internet, newspapers) • The writer mentions positive and negative aspects of the media • All age groups access a form of media • The writer emphasises how long people spend using the media **+ a relevant example which must back up their reason** eg: • The young people access media online and older people read newspapers • They need the media to find out what is going on around the world • People watch news which can be educational but celebrities find the media intrusive • The writer suggests that celebrity magazines/reality TV are an escape from everyday life • The writer says that French people spend a minimum of three hours watching television Assertion + reason = 1 mark Supporting **linking/relevant** examples = 1 mark

Question 9 – Translation

The translation into English is allocated 10 marks. The text for translation will be divided into a number of sense units. Each sense unit is worth 2 marks, which will be awarded according to the quality and accuracy of the translation into English.

1	2 marks available:
Juliette Morelle qui prend le train tous les jours observe	Juliette Morelle who takes the train every day observes
Juliette Morelle qui prend le train	Juliette Morelle who takes/uses/gets the train
tous les jours	every day/on a daily basis
observe	observes/observed (stylistic expression)
	notes
	1 mark:
	Omission of who travels/goes by train
	and observes/watches
	0 marks:
	took
	Omission of every day
	all the days
	had observed/will observe/sees/to observe/any other tense

2	2 marks available:
«On voit les jeunes partout taper sur leur tablette	"One sees/you see young people everywhere (typing) on their tablet(s)
«On voit	"One sees/you see/we see
les jeunes	young people/youngsters
partout	everywhere
taper sur leur tablette	(typing/tapping/using) on their tablet(s)
	1 mark:
	Watch
	people/(the) youths/the youngsters/the young people/(the) teenagers
	always
	Omission of their
	0 marks:
	Omission of one/you/we see(s)
	saw (tense unless R.E.)
	to see
	watched
	children/infants
	Omission of everywhere
	banging/slamming/hitting
	put their tablets on
	all their tablets
	device(s)/phone(s)

3	2 marks available:
tout en regardant les émissions d'hier soir	while watching last night's programmes/shows
tout en regardant	while watching
les émissions	programmes/shows
d'hier soir	last night's/yesterday evening's/(the) programmes from the night before
	1 mark:
	all while
	Omission of while
	and watching the
	as they watch
	yesterday night
	0 marks:
	always/all
	to watch
	all (in) watching
	as they watched
	Omission of last night/evening
	emissions/channels

4	2 marks available:
qu'ils ont téléchargées.	(which/that) they (have) downloaded
	1 mark:
	which they had downloaded
	0 marks:
	are downloading/that are downloadable/they would download
	Position of last night eg they downloaded last night

5	2 marks available:
Je dois dire que le bruit incessant m'énerve énormément. »	I have to say (that) the incessant noise annoys me enormously/greatly."
Je dois dire que	I have to/must say (that)
le bruit incessant	the incessant/the unceasing/the constant/the non-stop/persistent/never-ending noise
m'énerve	annoys/irritates/bugs me/gets on my nerves
énormément. »	enormously/greatly/massively/hugely/tremendously/a great deal."
	1 mark:
	I need to say (that)/I must admit (that)
	a lot/really
	0 marks:
	inceasing/instantly
	Omission of incessant
	annoyed/enerves me
	edgy
	makes/puts me on edge
	environment

Directed Writing

Please refer to pages 90–92 for advice on the general marking principles for Higher French — Directing Writing.

Section 1 — Listening

Item 1

Question		Expected response(s)
1. (a)		• I am <u>no longer</u> a baby/I'm not a baby <u>anymore</u> • Holidays with the family are boring/they find them boring/it is boring • I miss my friends *(Any 2 from 3)*
(b)		• Take/make his/her/their <u>own</u> decisions • Make his/her/their <u>own</u> mistakes *NB It is acceptable to have 'own' once. For example 'make their own decisions and mistakes' = 2 marks*
(c)	(i)	• <u>Language/linguistic</u> holidays/trips • Staying with <u>a</u> family/holiday with <u>a</u> family *(Any 1 from 2)*
	(ii)	• Perfect/improve a language • Discover/experience/understand another/different/a new culture(s) *(Any 1 from 2)*
(d)		• <u>Feel</u> safe/secure/a <u>sense of</u> security • (Parents) <u>pay</u> for <u>everything</u>/everything is <u>paid</u> for OR • <u>Pay</u> for food/accommodation/activities (need 2 details)

Item 2

Question		Expected response(s)
2. (a)		• (She was very active and) she liked being outdoors/in the fresh air/outside • She was an only child/had no brothers or sisters <u>and</u> had nobody to play with OR • She was <u>less</u> alone/lonely/on her own
(b)	(i)	• Painting • (Playing) board games
	(ii)	• (Learn to) play <u>together</u> • (Learn to) work as a <u>team/teamwork/groupwork</u> *(Any 1 from 2)*
(c)		• She <u>helped</u> the <u>younger/youngest/young</u> ones/children/people • When they had problems/if they had problems/with problems/when they were homesick/when they missed their parents
(d)	(i)	• He did not talk/speak <u>much/a lot</u>/he <u>hardly/barely</u> talked/spoke • He did not <u>want</u> to take part/participate/join in (in the activities) *(Any 1 from 2)*
	(ii)	• She spent (a lot of) time with him • She talked/chatted/spoke to him a <u>lot/lots/often/frequently</u> *(Any 1 from 2)*

(e)		• She has a meeting/a get together/meets/gets together with <u>colleagues/(fellow/other) workers/leaders</u> OR • She discusses/plans/talks about/figures out the timetable/programme of activities <u>for the next day</u> • Supervise/look after/keep an eye on/watch the children at meal times or any specific meal/when they eat
(f)		• It is a region/area/place she does not know (at all)/is not familiar with • (She has learned Spanish and) is hoping/wishes/wants/would like to/will be able to/is able to/can go to Spain (during her holiday) *(Any 1 from 2)*

Section 2 — Writing

Please refer to pages 93–95 for advice on general marking principles for Higher French — Writing.